Virtues Reflection & Colouring Book

Marja van 't Wel

© 2015 ACT on Virtues Publishers

Text and illustrations
Marja van 't Wel

Cover and text design
Annelies Wiersma

Translation
Simone Prins Translations

Special thanks to
Sandra Davis

First published in 2012
© ACT on Virtues Publishers
and 't Palet

All rights reserved
ISBN 978 94 920940 49

Safe boundaries
Feel free to make copies for yourself so you may colour the giraffe in its true colours one time then in a colour of your choice in another. You are permitted to make copies of the pictures for workshops. If you do so, please refer to where the book can be purchased.
And please share your photos on our Facebook page.

Besides that: no part of this publication may be reproduced or republished without written permission of both the owner and the publisher of this book.

Please write to
Annelies Wiersma
info@actonvirtues.nl

Contents

5. Introduction

9. Reflection

Domestic (in Holland)

10. Donkey
12. Swan
14. Deer
16. Butterfly
18. Lamb
20. Kingfisher
22. Horse
24. Snail
26. Beaver
28. Peacock
30. St. Bernard dog
32. Rooster
34. Sheep
36. Bee
38. Rabbit
40. Cow
42. Squirrel
44. Cat
46. Owl
48. Pig

Exotic (in Holland)

50. Eagle
52. Baboon
54. Bear
56. Dolphin
58. Flamingo
60. Gazelle
62. Giraffe
64. Camel
66. Kangaroo
68. Koala
70. Crocodile
72. Jellyfish
74. Lion
76. Elephant
78. Parrot
80. Penguin
82. Prairie dog
84. Turtle
86. Tiger
88. Wolf

90. Space for notes

95. Share experiences

96. Virtues The Gifts of Character
    (list of 100 virtues)

Introduction

Did you ever think of learning about determination from a Donkey? Patience from a Turtle? Reverence from a Bear? The animals in this unique colouring book bring out our hidden qualities; the inner virtues that are an enormous source of wisdom within each of us.

How the idea of this book came about

Mary, a chronically ill friend of art therapist Marja van 't Wel who has to go to hospital on a regular basis, mentioned to Marja that doing crossword puzzles and reading magazines was becoming rather boring!

Marja came up with the perfect solution: a colouring book! Due to this idea and Marja's magnificent and inspiring drawings, colouring is now all the craze in Holland. More and more people and countries are getting infected with it.

Why? Colouring is a creative and meaningful activity that gives inspiration. We all did it at some stage of our lives. Why ever stop? You don't have to be a top artist to get great results. It is never the same and always personal.

With her friend in mind, Marja set to work. She drew a set of animal outline images that would allow her friend to add her own colours. Each animal image also came with a set of reflection questions. This makes this colouring activity unique, when compared to other colouring books. Besides being relaxing and creative, it is also inspiring and meaningful. 'Close to nature', and close to "our nature", according to Marja.

Marja's friend Mary enjoyed the activity immensely. Reflecting on the questions and balancing the virtues was really supportive for her. She encouraged Marja to develop more images and to share the activity with others. That is how this book was developed.

Today, Marja's magnificent books are not only enjoyed by individuals, but also by people that regularly meet in groups to colour. The books are used in schools, hospitals and retirement homes: everywhere where people like to spend time on personal and spiritual development.

How it works: the animal coaches

This book contains images of animals that can function as animal coaches. Every animal has qualities that are unique to it. Think of the Kangaroo and the Turtle. One is fast moving and the other is slower moving. Or the Bee and the Pig. We associate the Bee with diligence; the Pig with laziness. But be careful to put labels on animal (read human) behaviour. Diligence can easily exhaust one when driven by perfectionism. And laziness can be really necessary when you are close to a burn-out. What we know is that every type of behaviour fulfils a need and is driven by our belief system. And that some may find it easier to practise a certain virtue than others. We are all unique. And able to learn from our experiences.

The process of colouring and reflecting will provide you with the opportunity to access some of these hidden beliefs and the intentions behind them. The animal that you choose to colour can mirror and give you insights into your behaviour. And maybe provide a learning opportunity: the opportunity to grow or balance one or more virtues. Especially if you are prepared to be honest with yourself and open to the intention behind the animal's qualities.

We hope you will enjoy it, and that it will give you colourful moments and inspiration.

Some tips before you start
(more on www.facebook.com/virtuescolouringandreflectionbook)

- Many people experience the art of 'colouring in' as a relaxing, fun and even therapeutic activity. Everyone can do it. You don't have to be an artist or even inspired or motivated to create something, as the images and lines are already there. It also works if you have a low energy level, as it doesn't require a lot of effort.

- Is this the first time that you are adding colour to a picture? Was it a long time ago? Before you start to colour your animal picture you may want to read these tips.

- You can choose an animal that 'speaks' to you, or pick any animal. Whatever you prefer.

- You can start with questioning yourself (for 2-3 minutes, or as long as you like):

    - What is this animal's strength?
    - What might be its growth virtue (a virtue it may develop)?
    - What do I recognise in the behaviour of this animal (strength, challenge)?
    - What message could this animal have for me?

- Once you have reflected on these questions, you can start to colour in your animal and afterwards do the reflection questions. It is absolutely fine if you want to work in a different order. Some people like to go over the reflection questions quickly or do them when they get stuck in the colouring.

- You can just enjoy colouring in your picture, and look at the reflection questions quickly, or you can reflect and go as deep as you like. Surprise yourself and see what happens. And please mind your own boundaries.

- You can colour in a realistic way, or in an intuitive way.

- You can start with colouring the animal, or the environment.

- Mind how you colour: is it with strength? Or softly? Bright colours or pastel?

- Be mindful about what emotions you are experiencing: peace, enthusiasm, purposefulness, resistance, flow …

- You might want to keep a log of what you are experiencing.

- You may want to use colours that go well together: pink/orange/yellow, or blue/purple/green …

- If you colour lightly, you can use colours over each other, mixing them to make a new colour.

- If you know about the meaning of colours you can use this too, as red is for passion, orange for creativity, purple for spirituality … Pink represents friendliness. There are many websites and books that can teach you about the meaning of colours.

- Remember that you do not need to stay inside the lines! And maybe you like to add things, like a rainbow, flower or bee …

- It is not necessary to colour in the whole picture. Leaving parts uncoloured is fine!

- We encourage you to do this activity 'by yourself and in silence', even when you are with a group. This will bring a meditative quality to the process and allow for a meditation atmosphere.

- You may put on soft music, it can be helpful to come in a meditative mood.

- After approximately an hour of colouring, you can start to share experiences.

Virtues Reflection Cards

You may want to use this book together with the 'Virtues Reflection Cards' from Linda Kavelin-Popov. She is one of the founders of the worldwide Virtues Project™.

The set of 100 full colour cards features photographs of natural beauty from around the globe. The in-depth descriptions of the virtues are based on research into the world's diverse sacred traditions. They are written for adults to use in daily reflection. A Virtues Pick, either in a sharing circle or in your own quiet time, helps to focus more deeply on cultivating the virtues.

Reviewers have called them "sacred", "exquisite", "a guide to life". The sets are available through www.virtuesproject.com or in Dutch through www.actonvirtues.nl

Programs and materials of The Virtues Project™

To order more copies of The Virtues Reflection & Colouring Book or other virtues materials, visit the on line shop at www.virtuesproject.com

Also available: Linda Kavelin-Popov's books 'A Pace of Grace; the Virtues of a Sustainable Life' and 'Graceful Endings, Navigating the Journey of Loss and Grief', 'The Family Virtues Guide' and Annelies Wiersma's book 'Raising Children with the Virtues, Bring out the best in your child and yourself' and virtue cards and books for children and young adults.

Reflection

*I never thought that colouring a colouring picture
would affect me this much.*

*I opened the book on the page with the rooster.
Its dominant, macho behaviour goes against the grain with me.*

*But I got down to it all the same.
I felt increasingly attached to this animal,
and spent close to two hours on colouring.*

*In the meantime, I pondered over the reflection questions.
The rooster gave me an important insight:
it is alright for me to stand up for myself,
to make myself be heard.*

*I often take a far too modest position.
The reflection and colouring has boosted my confidence
and now I am no longer afraid to step into the limelight.*

It took a rooster to make me see this!

Gwen, the Netherlands

The Donkey

Donkeys are brave, quiet, smart, determined, loyal and cautious. They have a good memory. There's no making a donkey drink against his will. People often think that donkeys are stupid and stubborn, but that is a misconception.

Reflection questions

- What do you think is the difference between stubbornness and determination?
- Do you finish what you started, or do you give up quickly?
- Does determination lead to growth or to stagnation?
- What in your life requires your determination at this moment?
- In what kind of situations do you demonstrate flexibility?
- What lesson does the donkey teach you?

....
....
....
....
....
....

The Swan

Swans are monogamous and faithful. A couple stays together for life. While the female sits on her nest, hatching the eggs, the male stands guard. Swans can be pretty argumentative. Sometimes they temporarily separate to give each other some space. Only to meet up later to continue their relationship in harmony.

Reflection questions

- How important is loyalty/faithfulness in your life?
- How loyal are you when things become difficult in relationships?
- Who or what requires your faithfulness and commitment?
- How can you be faithful to yourself and keep your own integrity?
- Do you feel that you have to make sacrifices to be faithful, or does it enrich your life?
- What lesson does the swan teach you?

....

....

....

....

....

....

The Deer

Deer have long, slender legs, large ears and soft, velvety eyes on the sides of the skull. The nostrils are large; they vibrate to sniff the smell of danger. The deer is alert and able to respond quickly.

Reflection questions

- How do you respond to people and circumstances around you?
- How does it show, physically (in your body), mentally (in your head) and emotionally (in your heart)?
- How can you protect yourself against threats to your well-being?
- When do you just know that something is good or bad for you?
- In what ways do you make use of your (high) sensitivity and intuition?
- What lesson does the deer teach you?

....

....

....

....

....

....

The Butterfly

The butterfly is a symbol of idealism, transformation and happiness. Butterflies begin their life as a larva, they pupate and transform into winged and colourful creatures. That process of transformation is something the butterfly has to go through independently.

Reflection questions

- What would you like to change in your life?
- How colourful can you be within the confines of what is possible for you?
- What would be the perfect moment to leave the cocoon and fly away?
- What do you need to get out of your cocoon?
- When is the best time to turn into a caterpillar again?
- What lesson does the butterfly teach you?

....

....

....

....

....

....

The Lamb

The lamb likes to be close to its mother. You can see it jumping and frolicking in the meadow. Sometimes it wants to leave the group to explore the world. Its mother then corrects and protects it.

Reflection questions

- What do you do to play and relax?
- Innocence and frankness; when is this a favour and when an escape/trap?
- From whom do you accept correction?
- Do you experience enough joy, or could you use more fun in your life?
- Who or what do you need to look for – or stay away from – to find joy in your life?
- What lesson does the lamb teach you?

....

....

....

....

....

....

....

The Kingfisher

In a straight, fast flight the kingfisher skims the surface of the water, completely focused on its goal. Its feathers are a magnificent bright azure blue and a fiery orange.

Reflection questions

- What would you like to focus on in the near future?
- Which virtues could you use to reach your goal?
- Which virtues could you develop further?
- What are the obstacles you might encounter? How will you tackle them?
- What kind of help or support do you need?
- What lesson does the kingfisher teach you?

The Horse

The horse has a strong temperament and character. He is forceful and headstrong but also gentle, elegant and noble. He understands the language of feelings. You have to earn a horse's respect and trust to get close to it.

Reflection questions

- Which virtues of the horse do you find inspiring? In what way?
- In what kind of situations do you tighten the reins? And when do you let go?
- What happens when you do either?
- How easy or difficult is it for others to gain your trust?
- Do you prefer to take the lead, or to follow suit?
- What lesson does the horse teach you?

....

....

....

....

....

....

The Snail

The snail is a boneless animal. It is soft-bodied, cold and moist. On its slow journey it occasionally lifts up its head, wondering where it is heading. Meanwhile, it indulges in eating leaves and plants and it leaves behind a (slimy) mark/reminder of its presence.

Reflection questions

- What does it feel like to be unable to move forward at your desired pace?
- When is your patience being challenged?
- In what kind of situations do you benefit from being patient?
- What is currently requiring you to be patient or testing your patience right now?
- How do you keep from becoming sluggish?
- What lesson does the snail teach you?

....

....

....

....

....

....

....

The Beaver

The beaver is the largest rodent in Europe. Usually five or six beavers live in a group, consisting of an adult couple and their young from their two latest litters. The beaver is known as a diligent worker, a builder of lodges and dams.

Reflection questions

- In what way could you see yourself as a builder of bridges? Try to illustrate your answer with an example.

- Do you like to cooperate with others or do you prefer to work alone?

- Which unique talents do you have to offer to a group?

- What talents of others complement your own?

- How does cooperation affect your energy flow?

- What lesson does the beaver teach you?

....

....

....

....

....

....

The Peacock

The peacock loves to parade - on the farm, in the park and in the zoo. The feathers of the male are absolutely stunning, and the peacock seems to be aware of its beauty. Its attitude seems arrogant; you can hear its voice from afar. Yet its appearance draws our admiration.

Reflection questions

- How does it feel for you to be the centre of attention?
- How do you feel about not being the centre of attention?
- How much do you appreciate your unique qualities?
- Do you have an arrogant streak or do you tend to be modest?
- What is it in your life that you are the most proud of?
- What lesson does the peacock teach you?

....

....

....

....

....

....

The St. Bernard Dog

The St. Bernard dog is an imposing dog. In the mountains he was used for detection and rescue work. The St. Bernard is a reliable guard dog as well. He will rarely let you down.

Reflection questions

- When will you be called upon as a rescuer?
- Is that a heavy responsibility for you, or is it something you can handle easily?
- When does rescuing become meddling?
- In what way does rescuing fulfil a need in you?
- How does it make you feel when others no longer need your protection?
- What lesson does the St. Bernard dog teach you?

....
....
....
....
....
....
....

The Rooster

The rooster is the 'guy' amongst the 'chick(en)s'. He does not tolerate other roosters in his vicinity. He takes pride in his colourful plumage, which he uses to impress 'the ladies' whenever he gets the chance. Roosters rarely lose sight of their goals and they don't give up.

Reflection questions

- How 'present' are you when you are with others?
- Are you a dominant person or do you let others dominate you?
- Dominance or decisiveness: what is the difference to you?
- How does authoritative behaviour or 'rooster behaviour' affect you?
- In what kind of situations is decisiveness expected or needed from you?
- What lesson does the rooster teach you?

....

....

....

....

....

....

The Sheep

A sheep moves forward with its flock. Backward steps cause sheep to become confused and uncertain. Sheep are kept on the moorlands to eat away the grass and saplings that grow between the heather plants. Sheep's wool isolates well and functions as a natural air conditioner.

Reflection questions

- How obedient and docile are you?
- What kind of situations can start things to fester under your skin?
- Are you open to change or do you prefer to hold on to "the old way"?
- Who would you, so to speak, follow 'blindly'?
- Which situation – or person – makes you feel confused or uncertain?
- What lesson does the sheep teach you?

....

....

....

....

....

....

The Bee

The worker bee spends its entire life extracting nectar to make honey, a very responsible task. The Queen bee lays eggs from December to October. Without her, the group falls apart and is no longer productive.

Reflection questions

- What activities do you currently engage in?
- Are they useful, compulsive or playful?
- How do you balance work and play?
- What do you demand from others?
- When do you feel contentment?
- What lesson does the bee teach you?

....
....
....
....
....
....
....

The Rabbit

The rabbit is often kept in a cage, but that is really not its way of living. A caged rabbit can become lethargic and sick from boredom. It likes to eat varied food, just a little of everything. It is also fond of new adventures. It can feel restless if there is little going on in its life.

Reflection questions

- How long does your contentment last? Or do you soon become bored?
- How often and when do you become restless?
- Where and how do you feel restless? Physically, mentally, or emotionally?
- When does your restlessness and hunger for new adventures become escapism?
- What could you do if you know you are avoiding things/not finishing things?
- What lesson does the rabbit teach you?

....

....

....

....

....

....

The Cow

The cow is a curious herd animal. Cows on a farm are milked twice a day. Usually a cow does not show much initiative, and it can be quite stubborn. After the birth of a calf, the cow cleans her newborn with her tongue and stimulates it to stand on its own legs.

Reflection questions

- Are you a generous giver or do you find it difficult to share?

- How do you rate yourself when it comes to warmth, gentleness and friendship?

- Are there limits to your generosity or do you let people take advantage of you? (a cow that gives too much milk might run dry)

- What about your expectations of others if you give something away?

- How steadfast do you stand - are you quick to be of service to others?

- What lesson does the cow teach you?

....

....

....

....

....

....

The Squirrel

The squirrel feeds on plant material, such as nuts and seeds of spruce and pine trees. It prepares itself with a sense of purpose and care for the winter months. In winter the squirrel can take a rest and benefit from what is has collected. On bleak days it hides in its nest.

Reflection questions

- How well-stocked is your store room?

- How do you keep your energy levels up?

- Do you store things that you no longer need?

- Can you enjoy a simple biscuit as much as patisserie?

- When is it the right time to part with things that have become a burden to you?

- What lesson does the squirrel teach you?

....

....

....

....

....

....

The Cat

Many people think that the cat is a solitary animal and that it does not need company. That is a misconception. Cats like to sleep together and they like to sit near each other. When a cat and a dog live together, they can tolerate each other or even enjoy having each other around.

Reflection questions

- When do you need company?
- When do you need solitude?
- Do you find it hard or easy to 'fit in' with people?
- How can you develop tolerance without forcing yourself?
- How do you create a win-win situation within a relationship?
- What lesson does the cat teach you?

The Owl

The owl is a nocturnal animal. It has a silent observation skill, a sharp eyesight and good sense of hearing. It has an impressive ability to rotate its head. It evaluates a situation before it responds with a course of action.

Reflection questions

- How do you evaluate a situation?
- Do you prefer to sit back and observe or do you prefer to take action?
- How much do you rely on your own wisdom?
- How willing are you to listen to the wisdom of others?
- If you could choose between following your own wisdom and listening to others, what option would you prefer?
- What lesson does the owl teach you?

....
....
....
....
....
....
....

The Pig

The pig is an intelligent, curious, relatively clean and social animal. It may seem lazy, but that is because it is mostly active at dusk and at night. It likes to dig around in the soil with its sensitive snout. The domestic pig will eat anything it is given.

Reflection questions

- What makes you oink? (Happy and content)

- Sitting, eating, drinking, sleeping and playing is a way of life.
  What would that be like for you?/How would that work for you?

- What situations do you tend to neglect?

- Can you leave things as they are, let go, lean back and enjoy life?
  Are you capable of that?

- What do you think: can laziness lead to a happy and fulfilling life?

- What lesson does the pig teach you?

....

....

....

....

....

....

....

The Eagle

The eagle is a large bird of prey with broad wings, sharp claws and a sturdy beak. Of all birds the eagle can fly the highest. It has an extraordinary eyesight and overview.

Reflection questions

- Looking back on your life from a distance, what were important life experiences you have had?

- Who were your role models and why?

- What are you grateful for?

- What would you take with you on your flight, and what will you leave behind?

- What insights did you have that, when applied, made a positive difference?

- What lesson does the eagle teach you?

....

....

....

....

....

....

The Baboon

Baboons live in groups. They flea each other and they play together. This is how they form mutual bonds. They also need space for themselves. Females, young ones and siblings form the stable centre of a group. The females stay together for life. Male baboons leave when they have reached maturity to move to another group.

Reflection questions

- What does friendship mean to you?
- With whom do you share a special bond? What do you get out of it?
- With whom do you like to play?
- How much time and energy do you spend on a friendship?
- How much space do you have/need for yourself?
- What lesson does the baboon teach you?

....
....
....
....
....
....
....

The Bear

The bear is mainly known for its strength and courage. Its thick pelt keeps it warm in winter. Its siblings are born during its hibernation. Some bears don't go into a long hibernation and only take a couple of days to 'rest' before becoming active again.

Reflection questions

- How much time do you take for personal reflection? What does it bring you?

- What needs your attention/reflection now?

- What is a good way for you to reach inner peace?

- How do you experience silence and loneliness?

- What is a good period of the year for you to find balance?

- What lesson does the bear teach you?

....

....

....

....

....

....

The Dolphin

The mouth of a dolphin looks like it is smiling/laughing all the time. This makes it look friendly and open to communication. Dolphins like to play. Biologists have experienced that dolphins learn easily and quickly.

Reflection questions

- With whom can you have a good laugh?

- When was the last time that you had a good laugh?
  In what way was it helpful?

- How easily do you connect or communicate with others?

- What was the last new thing that you learned?

- How easily do you learn/pick up new things?

- What lesson does the dolphin teach you?

....

....

....

....

....

....

....

The Flamingo

Flamingos live in colonies in lagoons. They share the care for each other's offspring. Couples use their own language (call for each other with a special yell). Flamingos and storks often stand on one leg, perhaps to stop them from sinking into the mud.

Reflection questions

- How good are you at balancing, helping others and yourself?

- Is there a chance that you might 'sink into the mud', because there is too much work on your plate?

- What could you use help with right now?

- Who could you ask for help?

- How could you be of service to others?

- What lesson does the flamingo teach you?

....

....

....

....

....

....

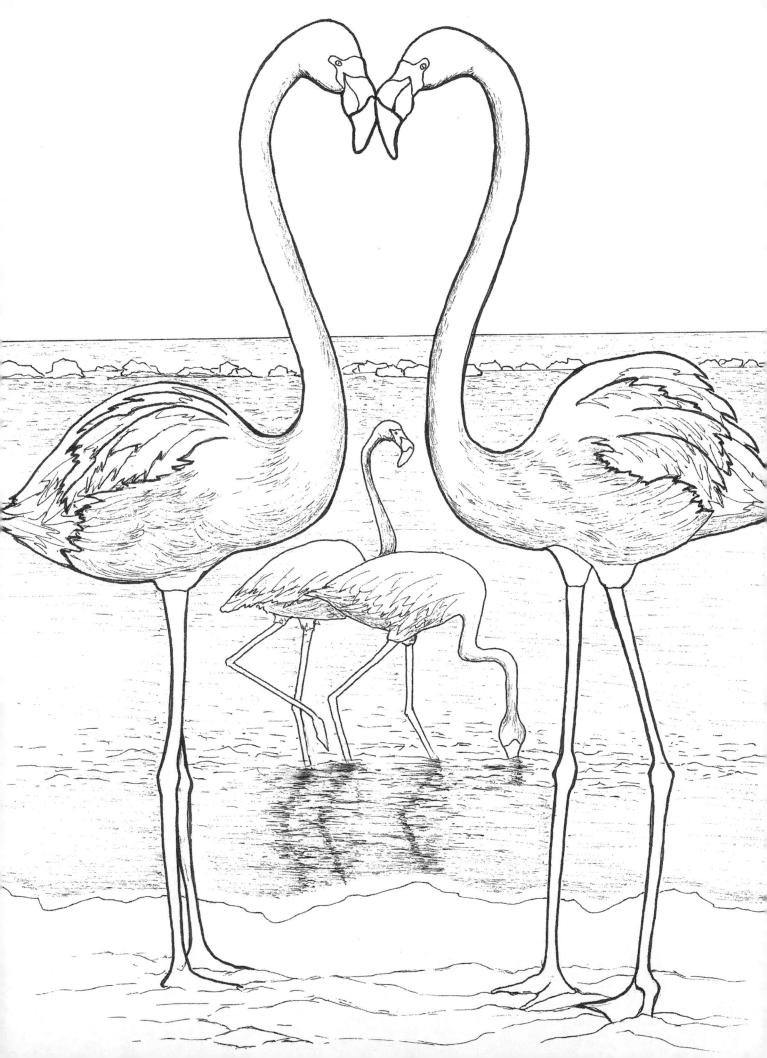

The Gazelle

Like most antelopes, the gazelle is a shy and peaceful animal. It trusts what it hears and smells and runs away when it is sensing danger. Or it protects itself with its sharp antlers (horns). The gazelle is still an easy prey for some predators. It does not form long-term relationships.

Reflection questions

- How do you respond when someone attacks you?
- How do you respond when someone criticises you?
- Do you run away? Or do you defend yourself?
- When do you choose to speak? And when do you keep your silence?
- Are your relationships with others long lasting, or do you prefer to hang around with people for short periods of time?
- What lesson does the gazelle teach you?

....

....

....

....

....

....

The Giraffe

Because of its very long neck, the giraffe is the tallest animal in the world. The giraffe is visible high above other animal species it lives with. It does not have many enemies; it has a sort of grace about it. The giraffe is most vulnerable when it is drinking as it bends over in a split.

Reflection questions

- When did you stick out your neck? What virtues did you demonstrate?

- How do you handle appreciation?

- How do experience a 'split' situation? What do you need for yourself?

- How do you communicate with others from your (high) position?

- What do you do to stay connected with others?

- What lesson does the giraffe teach you?

....

....

....

....

....

....

....

The Camel

The camel lives in the desert. It is known for its endurance. It can go without water for weeks and it is resistant to very high and very low temperatures. The camel is a survivor. It is also known for its resilience and calmness. After hard times it can recover quickly. The camel is called 'The ship of the desert'.

Reflection questions

- When is/was your endurance being challenged?
- What sort of signals do you receive from your body?
- How do you bear times of deprivation and changes?
- Which virtues support/encourage endurance?
- What is the bright side of hard times you are/were going through?
- What lesson does the camel teach you?

....

....

....

....

....

....

The Kangaroo

The kangaroo is a great jumper. It can jump high and far and moves forward at high speed. The female kangaroo even jumps with her baby in her pouch. Because of their fast speed, kangaroos are not always aware of danger.

Reflection questions

- Big jumps, fast at the finish. Do you recognise that?
- What do you enjoy (or admire in people) in moving forward fast?
- What might happen when you go too fast?
- Do you like to haul others along in this fast-paced life?
- How can you respond to a fast 'kangaroo' if you find it hard to keep up with him/her?
- What lesson does the kangaroo teach you?

....

....

....

....

....

....

....

The Koala

The koala bear lives in Australia. It is one of the best-sleeping animals in the world. It has the ability to sleep for up to 22 hours per twenty-four hours. The remaining hours it is looking for food or social contact. The koala also needs time for itself. It can be defensive of its territory.

Reflection questions

- Are you more of a social animal or more of a loner?

- When do you feel the need for isolation?
  Or when do you feel the need for socialising?

- Do you have enough time for yourself, or could you use more space for yourself?

- What does "space for yourself" bring you?
  And what does socialising bring you?

- What do you do to balance the two opposites?

- What lesson does the koala teach you?

....

....

....

....

....

....

....

The Crocodile

The crocodile has a strong will to survive. With its powerful jaws it can cause major damage. Most animals and people are afraid of the crocodile. The body of the crocodile is covered with hard scales. The vulnerable part is its stomach.

Reflection questions

- Who or what is frightening you?

- In what situations do you feel irritated or even become aggressive?

- How does aggressive behaviour affect you?

- How do you handle emotions? Do your tears flow easily when you are seized with emotion; happy or sad, or is it hard for you to express yourself?

- When was the last time that you had a good, releasing cry?

- What lesson does the crocodile teach you?

....

....

....

....

....

....

The Jellyfish

The jellyfish is a transparent, blue, purple or brown invertebrate. It rolls on top of the waves and it goes with the flow - the low and the high tide. When it washes onto the shore, it remains motionless.

Reflection questions

- How clear and transparent are you in your communication?
- Can you easily get into "the flow", or is your flow dependent on others?
- Do you like to go with the flow, or against it?
- Do you have people near you that consume your energy?
- What can you do about that?
- What lesson does the jellyfish teach you?

....
....
....
....
....
....
....

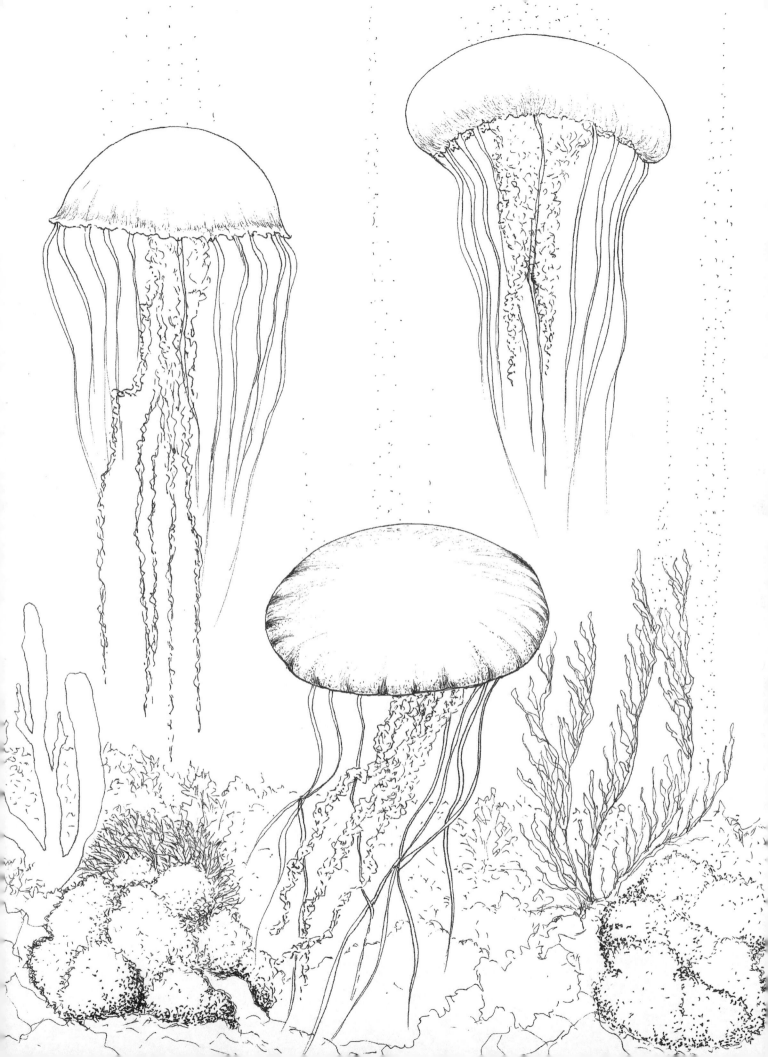

The Lion

The lion not only lives for itself, it also protects its clan. Its highly developed senses are on edge. It patiently waits for the attack until the moment is inevitable. When lions are relaxed, they can lie in the sun for days, only getting into action at twilight.

Reflection questions

- How do you respond when someone or something you love is attacked?
- How do you leap into action when you become alerted?
- What is the difference between suspicion and alertness?
- What do you need to be able to trust in a 'healthy' way?
- In what situations do you "fight" or "take flight"?
- What lesson does the lion teach you?

The Elephant

The elephant is known as a powerful, intelligent, understanding and social animal with an excellent memory. He is respected for his primeval strength and stability. On the savannah he follows a straight path without getting distracted. He clears the way for others.

Reflection questions

- When have you needed primeval strength?
- What gives your life stability?
- How do you keep on track?
- What traces or foot prints do you leave behind?
- What are the obstacles in your life right now that you wish to remove?
- What lesson does the elephant teach you?

....

....

....

....

....

....

The Parrot

The parrot is a colourful bird. It can draw attention with its penetrating call. It is a social animal. Parrots form couples in a group. The parrot is known to be talkative, but it has not been proven whether it understands what it is saying or whether it is just parroting.

Reflection questions

- What about your need for attention?
- How do you get attention?
- How present and thoughtful are you to others?
- Do you like to talk or do you prefer to listen?
- What is the difference between having a conversation and chattering?
- What lesson does the parrot teach you?

....

....

....

....

....

....

The Penguin

The female emperor penguin lays her egg on the ice far from the sea and, after that, immediately leaves for the sea. The male penguins hatch out the eggs during two extremely cold months. During these months they don't eat and lose a lot of weight. They stick close together, to stay warm.

Reflection questions

- Who do you give shelter to?
- How do you feel in a group?
- Have you ever felt left out in the cold? How did it feel?
- When do you feel lonely or left on your own, who is there for you?
- Do you easily show generosity or do you find it difficult to share?
- What lesson does the penguin teach you?

....

....

....

....

....

....

....

The Prairie Dog

The prairie dog isn't an actual dog, it's a rodent. It's a very social animal; you will rarely spot one on its own. The prairie dog is an easy prey for a lot of predators, which it is why it is often seen sitting on the ground with its head high in the sky.

Reflection questions

- What nibbles on you when you say "yes" but mean "no"?

- Do you do what you want to do yourself or do you do what other people expect you to do?

- How easy or hard is it for you to say "no"?

- What is your physical, mental and emotional reaction when someone crosses your boundaries?

- Which situations in your life ask for clear and safe boundaries?

- What lesson does the prairie dog teach you?

....

....

....

....

....

....

The Turtle

Turtles are often seen as slow animals. In reality, they can leg it quite fast and swim to safety quickly, even though they can't maintain such speeds for long. When danger lurks around the corner, turtles will pull their heads back into their shells for protection, waiting for the danger to pass.

Reflection questions

- When do you pull your head back into your shield?
- What does your shield look like? Thick, thin, hard, soft, big, small?
- What reasons do you have for retreating into your shell?
- What does it bring you, in a positive and negative way?
- When will you reappear again?
- What lesson does the turtle teach you?

....

....

....

....

....

....

....

The Tiger

The tiger is a catlike animal that can weigh up to three hundred kilograms and can reach a length of up to three metres. It can reach speeds of fifty kilometres per hour and swim ten kilometres in one go. His roar can be heard from four kilometres away. When a tiger is hungry he can devour a meal of up to twenty-five kilos. After that it will not feel hungry for several days.

Reflection questions

- What do you do to stay in shape and to feel healthy?
- Which habits are – to be honest with yourself - bad for your health?
- What kinds of things have positive influences on your health?
- How can you enjoy and live a healthy life?
- Do you mostly use a slow pace or fast pace in life and does this suit you?
- What lesson does the tiger teach you?

....

....

....

....

....

....

The Wolf

Wolves live in packs, led by a male and a female couple. The wolf knows a lot of ways to communicate, including facial expressions. The wolf howls to keep the pack together, or to let other wolfs know where it is. The howling can be heard up to ten kilometres away.

Reflection questions

- Do you keep quiet or do you let yourself be heard?

- How much of an effort does it take to let yourself be heard?

- Do you discourage/scare people with your sounds and language, or do other people discourage you?

- How do you respond to injustice or to disagreement?

- Do you feel heard or do you cry inside your "inner chamber"?

- What lesson does the wolf teach you?

....

....

....

....

....

....

....

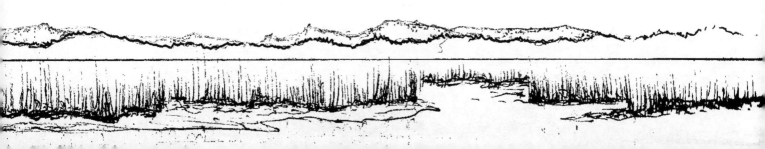

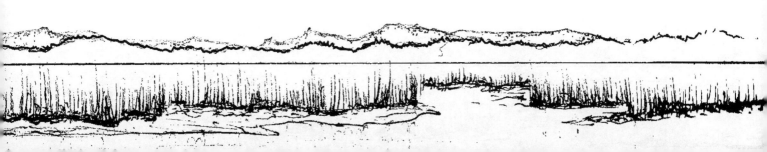

Share experiences

Marja van 't Wel

Please feel free to contact Marja van 't Wel: marjavantwel@gmail.com or through her website www.hetpalet.net. Marja loves to hear how you like her book and is willing to give personal advise.

Safe boundaries

Feel free to make copies for yourself, for instance to be able to colour the giraffe in its true colours AND in pink, OR green.
It is also allowed to make copies of the pictures for workshops. If you do so, please refer to where the book can be purchased.

Besides that: no part of this publication may be reproduced or republished without written permission of both the owner and the publisher of this book. Please write to Annelies Wiersma, info@actonvirtues.nl

Facebook

We would love to hear about your experiences with our book! Please share these experiences and photos of your pictures coloured in on our special Facebook page: www.facebook.com/virtuescolouringandreflectionbook

VIRTUES: The Gifts of Character

Acceptance
Accountability
Appreciation
Assertiveness
Awe
Beauty
Caring
Certitude
Charity
Cheerfulness
Cleanliness
Commitment
Compassion
Confidence
Consideration
Contentment
Cooperation
Courage
Courtesy
Creativity
Decisiveness
Detachment
Determination
Devotion
Dignity
Diligence
Discernment
Empathy
Endurance
Enthusiasm
Excellence
Fairness
Faith

Faithfulness
Fidelity
Flexibility
Forbearance
Forgiveness
Fortitude
Friendliness
Generosity
Gentleness
Grace
Gratitude
Helpfulness
Honesty
Honour
Hope
Humanity
Humility
Idealism
Independence
Initiative
Integrity
Joyfulness
Justice
Kindness
Love
Loyalty
Mercy
Mindfulness
Moderation
Modesty
Nobility
Openness
Optimism
Orderliness

Patience
Peacefulness
Perceptiveness
Perseverance
Prayerfulness
Purity
Purposefulness
Reliability
Resilience
Respect
Responsibility
Reverence
Righteousness
Sacrifice
Self-discipline
Serenity
Service
Simplicity
Sincerity
Steadfastness
Strength
Tact
Thankfulness
Thoughtfulness
Tolerance
Trust
Trustworthiness
Truthfulness
Understanding
Unity
Wisdom
Wonder
Zeal

Books and Virtues Reflection Cards are also available at a quantity discount. Please contact www.virtuesproject.com

Made in the USA
San Bernardino, CA
10 June 2016